Wildlife Watchers

Plants

Terry Jennings

QED Publishing

Copyright © QED Publishing 2009

First published in the UK in 2009 by
QED Publishing
A Quarto Group Company
226 City Road
London EC1V 2TT
www.qed-publishing.co.uk

ISBN 978 1 84835 235 3

Author Terry Jennings
Consultant Steve Parker
Project Editor Eve Marleau
Designer and Picture Researcher
    Liz Wiffen

Publisher Steve Evans
Creative Director Zeta Davies
Managing Editor Amanda Askew

Printed and bound
in China

The words in **bold**
are explained in the
glossary on page 30.

Contents

What is a flower?

Most plants have flowers. They come in many shapes and sizes. Some smell like beautiful perfume, but a few smell horrible. All flowers have the same job. They make seeds so that new plants can grow.

The parts of a flower

Most flowers have male and female parts. The male parts are called **stamens** and they produce tiny grains of yellow dust, called **pollen**. The female parts are called **carpels**. They are made up of a **stigma**, a **style** and an **ovary**. The egg-cells are made in the ovaries. A new seed is made after a pollen grain joins with an egg-cell. This is called **fertilization**.

Stigma
Style
STAMEN (male)
CARPEL (female)

Ovary

⬆ This lily flower has very large stamens and a large carpel in the middle of it.

Separate male and female plants

Not all plants have their male and female parts in the same flower. For example, there are separate male and female holly trees. Each tree has either male flowers or female flowers, but not both. Hazel trees have male and female flowers on the same tree.

Male holly flowers

Female holly flowers

Petals and sepals

There are other parts to most flowers, such as **petals**. Underneath the flower there are leaf-like parts called **sepals**.

Did you know?

The male flower of the birch tree is called a catkin. Each catkin can make more than five million pollen grains, which then blow away in the wind.

Petal

Sepal

Plant life

Many flowers are brightly coloured to attract insects and other animals to them. These animals are important, because they carry pollen from one flower to another.

↓ As this bee reaches into the flower to feed on nectar, pollen grains stick to its body.

Pollen

The importance of insects

A plant's egg-cells are usually fertilized by pollen from another plant of the same kind. Many flowers produce a sweet juice, called **nectar**, to attract animal pollen-carriers.

When an animal pushes into the flower to feed, pollen grains from the stamens stick to its body. On its visit to the next flower, some pollen may rub off onto the stigma. This is called **pollination**. A tiny tube grows down from the pollen grain into one of the egg-cells, and the egg-cell starts to grow into a seed. This is called fertilization.

Did you know?

Sometimes, the perfumes that flowers produce seem lovely to us. However, a few smell awful. The Rafflesia plant of Southeast Asia has the largest and smelliest flowers in the world.

↓ Catkins are the male flowers of hazel trees.

Going with the wind

Not all flowers are pollinated by insects or other animals. The wind spreads pollen between certain flowers, particularly those of grasses and many trees. These flowers are usually dull green and most do not have petals. They do not produce nectar or scent because they do not need to attract bees and other insects.

← These maple seeds have special 'wings' that help them to move with the wind.

7

Be a plant spotter

Some parts of plants are small, so you need to get close to see all their details. One way is to collect them. Another way is to use a magnifying glass. The most important equipment you need is your eyes.

➡ **U**se plastic scissors to collect cuttings of plants.

The plant-spotter's collecting kit

Here is the equipment you will need to become a plant spotter:

- Magnifying glass to see all the details of the plant
- Plastic bags to store your finds until you get home
- Small envelopes for collecting seeds
- Sticky labels
- Plastic scissors
- Small paintbrushes and tweezers to pick up small parts of plants
- Plant pots (or clean yoghurt pots)
- Trowel
- Some soil or compost
- Notebook to record your findings
- Pen or pencil
- Crayons

⬆ **A** magnifying glass lets you see small things much more clearly.

WARNING!

It is against the law to collect wild seeds, plants or flowers without permission from the owner of the land.

➡ **T**weezers are useful for picking up small parts of plants without damaging them.

➤ When you see a flower, draw a sketch in your notebook. You can add details about the flower's colours.

Keeping records

Every good plant spotter needs a notebook, some pencils and coloured crayons. Once you have found a flower, you could put the details in a table.

Date	Flower	Place	Where	Other flowers present	What was special about the flower?
3rd January	Snowdrop	Westacre Park	In lawn, in sun	None	Growing through the snow
11th February	Hazel catkins	Wymbarton Wood	Woodland	Celandines	Pollen blowing away in the wind

Did you know?

There are more than 250,000 different species, or kinds, of flowering plant in the world.

Weed winners

A weed is a plant that grows where it is not wanted. Weeds can grow so quickly that they flower and produce new seeds before you have noticed them. Some weeds have bright, colourful flowers.

Is my flower large and red in colour? Are my stamens black? Is my stem hairy?

Black stamens

Hairy stem

Spotting weeds

* Many weeds have a very short life cycle, from seeds to flowers and back to seeds again.

* Weeds produce a lot of seeds. Some of these seeds may stay hidden in the soil for many years until the conditions are right for them to grow.

* Some weeds have more than one way of surviving and spreading themselves. For example, if a dandelion plant is removed, some of its long root may stay in the soil. That piece of root will grow into a new plant.

Common or field poppy

Height: 20-60 cm
Size of flower: 7-10 cm
Flowers: Single flower on each stem
Habitat: Waste ground, roadsides, cornfields and farmland
Fruits or seeds: Seeds inside a hard, round fruit
Flowering time: Early summer

Tall spike

Am I tall with no hairs? Are there a lot of purple flowers growing in a spike out of the top of me?

Bright-yellow flower

Is my flower bright yellow? Does my flower stem have several branches on it?

Meadow buttercup

Height: 30-100 cm
Size of flower: 1.5-2.5 cm
Flowers: Single flower growing from each branch on the stem
Habitat: Grassland, meadows, grassy roadsides
Fruits or seeds: Group of small, dry seeds, each with a hooked tip
Flowering time: Spring/summer

Rosebay willowherb

Height: Up to 120 cm
Size of flower: 2-3 cm
Flowers: Many flowers growing in a cone shape at the top of the stem
Habitat: Bare or waste ground
Fruits or seeds: White, fluffy seeds
Flowering time: Summer/early autumn

Composite flowers

Some kinds of flower, such as daisies, are actually made up of hundreds of small flowers. They are called composite flowers. The small flowers form a flower head that looks like a single flower. Only the outer flowers have a single large petal.

Is my flower head small with white petals? Is the centre of my flower head yellow?

White petal

Yellow centre

Spotting composite plants

※ Some flowers, such as daisies, can open and close their flowers. As the sun sets, the flowers close up tightly. When the sun rises the next morning, the flowers slowly open again.

※ A dandelion flower head contains up to 200 tiny flowers. These close up at night or in bad weather.

※ The spear thistle is one of the best-protected plants. Each leaf ends in a spine.

Common daisy

Height: 7–15 cm
Size of flower: 1.5–3 cm
Flowers: One flower head on each stem
Habitat: Lawns, playing fields, meadows and roadsides
Fruits or seeds: Small, oval seeds with flat ends, covered in hair
Flowering time: Summer

Purple flower head

Is my flower head yellow? Do all of my tiny flowers have a petal?

Is my flower head purple? Am I tall? Are all my parts spiny?

Hairy seeds

Yellow flower head

Watch it!

Collect some seed heads of dandelion plants – they are called dandelion clocks. Blow on the clock. See how far the seeds travel on their parachutes.

Spiny parts

Dandelion

Height: 5–30 cm
Size of flower: 3–7.5 cm
Flowers: One flower head on each stem
Habitat: Lawns, grassland, waste ground and roadsides
Fruits or seeds: Each little seed has a 'parachute' of silky hairs, which helps the wind to carry it
Flowering time: Spring/autumn

Spear thistle

Height: 30–150 cm
Size of flower: 3–5 cm
Flowers: One, or a group of two or three flower heads, on a stem
Habitat: Fields, roadsides, waste ground
Fruits or seeds: Yellow seeds with black streaks, topped by a 'parachute' of white hairs
Flowering time: Late summer/ early autumn

13

Storing food

Some plants have special leaves or stems that are used to store food for winter. Then they will have plenty of food for when they start to grow again in spring. Some of these plants can make new copies of themselves without producing seeds.

? Does my flower have a yellow trumpet? Does it have quite a few petals and sepals?

Yellow trumpet shape

Spotting food-storing plants

❀ A daffodil flower grows from a **bulb**. This is made up of fleshy leaves that are full of food, which is used by the growing shoot.

❀ A crocus grows from a **corm**. This is a round stem full of stored food.

❀ A potato is a swollen part of an underground stem, which will grow into a new plant if it is planted.

Daffodil

Height: 20–40 cm
Size of flower: 3.5–10 cm
Flowers: One flower on each flat stem
Habitat: Parks and gardens. Also grows wild in some woods and grassland areas
Fruits or seeds: Fruit splits into three parts when it is ripe, releasing small, brown seeds
Flowering time: Late spring

Drooping outer petals

Am I small with funnel-shaped flowers? Are my flowers white, purple, cream or yellow?

Flat stem

Are my flowers blue or yellow? Do I have three drooping outer petals? Do I have a flat stem?

Funnel-shaped flower

Flag iris

Height: 40–150 cm
Size of flower: 8–12 cm
Flowers: 2–3 flowers on a stem
Habitat: Gardens and parks. Also grows wild in ditches, ponds, marshes and near rivers
Fruits or seeds: Brown seeds in a pod that splits open into three parts
Flowering time: Late spring/summer

Crocus

Height: Less than 10 cm
Size of flower: 2–4 cm
Flowers: One on each stem
Habitat: Parks and gardens. It grows wild in some areas
Fruits or seeds: Small seeds inside a three-sided fruit
Flowering time: Late winter/early spring

Watch it!

Every potato has several eyes, or buds, from which a new shoot will grow. Stand a potato on a sunny windowsill. Watch what happens to the 'eyes' over a few days.

Climbing plants

Am I woody with green leaves? Are my leaves heart shaped?

Plants need sunlight to make their food. Most plants grow upwards to get as much sunlight as possible. Climbing plants with weak stems cannot grow upwards on their own. They use other plants for support.

Heart-shaped leaves

Spotting climbing plants

* Ivy has tiny roots growing from its stems. These help it to scramble up a tree, fence or wall.

* Honeysuckle climbs by winding itself around young trees. Sometimes it squashes the trunk of the tree and makes it look like a corkscrew.

* The long, tough stems of brambles are armed with hooked prickles.

Ivy

Height: Up to 30 m on trees
Size of flower: 3-4 mm
Flowers: In groups
Habitat: On trees, cliffs, buildings, walls and fences
Fruits or seeds: Black fruit
Flowering time: Late autumn/ early winter

Woody stem

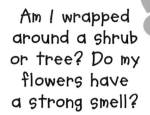

Am I wrapped around a shrub or tree? Do my flowers have a strong smell?

Are my flowers white or pink and do I have blackberries? Am I using sharp, hooked prickles to climb over other plants?

Blackberry fruit

Strong-smelling flower

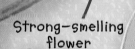

Blackberry or bramble

Height: Up to 3 m
Size of flower: 2-3 cm
Flowers: Single or in groups
Habitat: Hedgerows, meadows and woodland
Fruits or seeds: Blackberry fruits
Flowering time: Autumn

Honeysuckle

Height: Up to 6 m
Size of flower: 4-5 cm
Flowers: In clusters, or groups, all pointing outwards
Habitat: Woodland, hedgerows and planted in gardens
Fruits or seeds: Groups of red berries
Flowering time: Late summer/early autumn

Did you know?

The strangler fig is a climbing plant. It wraps itself around a tree and steals its water and food. Its leaves block the tree's sunlight, causing it to die.

Sharp, hooked prickle

17

Water plants

All plants need water so they can feed and grow. Water plants grow in places such as ponds, lakes, ditches and swamps. Some plants live in or under water, while others float on the water's surface.

Do I have large floating leaves? Are my flowers large and white, with 20–25 pointed petals?

Large petal

Spotting water plants

❀ Plants such as flag irises grow in the shallow water at the edges of ponds, rivers and streams. They have long, strong roots to fix them firmly in the mud.

❀ Plants such as water lilies and water crowfoot grow partly covered by water. These plants often have thin and bendy stems so that they can move with the water.

❀ The stems of some water plants have spaces for air in them. These help to hold the plants up in the water.

White water lily

Height: Grows in water to a depth of about 3 m
Size of flower: 10–20 cm
Flowers: Single flower on a long stem rising from the roots
Habitat: Still or slow-flowing water
Fruits or seeds: Ball-shaped fruits that float away
Flowering time: Summer/early autumn

Am I mostly underwater? Do I have small, white flowers with a yellow centre?

Yellow centre

Small, white petal

Watch it!

Mint is a water plant. Put a shoot of a mint plant in a bottle of water. Stand the bottle on a sunny windowsill. After a few days, the mint shoot will start to grow roots.

Water crowfoot

Height: Grows in water to a depth of 2.5–120 cm
Size of flower: 13 mm
Flowers: Single or in groups
Habitat: Ponds, streams, rivers and ditches
Fruits or seeds: Small, dry seeds
Flowering time: Summer

Yellow flower

Am I growing in water, but my roots are not in the soil? Are my yellow flowers above the surface of the water?

Bladderwort

Height: Grows in water to a depth of 15–45 cm
Size of flower: 12–18 mm
Flowers: 2–10 flowers on a long stem above the water
Habitat: Deep lakes and ponds
Fruits or seeds: Small, round fruits
Flowering time: Summer

WARNING!

You must always be with an adult near water.

19

Vital grasses

Grasses are probably the most important plants in the world. They provide food for animals and many of the foods we eat come from grass, too.

Do my flowers look flattened? Do they form a zig-zag pattern up my smooth stem?

Flattened flowers

Zig-zag pattern

Spotting grasses

❀ Although they are usually dull and green, grasses do have flowers. Grass flowers do not have petals or bright colours because they are pollinated by the wind.

❀ Grass species include wheat, oats, barley, rice and maize, which are made into foods such as breakfast cereals and bread.

❀ Grasses are food for many wild animals. In some places, such as the UK, straw or reeds are used to make the roofs of houses.

Perennial rye grass

Height: 10–90 cm
Size of flower: 4–5 mm
Flowers: 4–14 flowers in a zig-zag pattern up the stem
Habitat: Grassland, farms, waste ground
Fruits or seeds: Small, dry seeds
Flowering time: Late spring/early summer

Am I growing near water? Is my flower head soft and brown in colour?

Brown flower

Groups of flowers

Am I growing in a clump with other grass plants? Does my flower head have groups of many flowers?

Oat grass

Height: 50–150 cm
Size of flower: 4–6 mm
Flowers: In loose bunches
Habitat: Rough grassland, meadows, roadsides, hedgerows, and as a weed in corn crops
Fruits or seeds: Small, dry seeds
Flowering time: Summer

Reed grass

Height: 1.5–3 m
Size of flower: 4–6 mm
Flowers: In large groups
Habitat: Grows in thick clumps on the edges of ponds, lakes, rivers and marshes
Fruits or seeds: Small, dry seeds
Flowering time: Summer/autumn

Trees

A tree is a large, woody plant. Trees grow tall and the branches grow long. At the same time, the roots grow deeper. The tree trunk gets fatter each year as a new layer of wood grows just beneath the bark.

Spotting trees

🌼 Many trees shed their leaves each autumn – they are called **deciduous** trees. Not all trees shed their leaves at once – they are called **evergreens**.

🌼 There are about 100,000 different species of tree in the world.

🌼 Trees, such as plum and apple trees, have bright flowers that are pollinated by insects. However, most trees, such as oak, ash and maple, have flowers that are dull and green and are pollinated by the wind.

Oak

Height: Up to 35 m
Types of flower: Separate male and female flowers that are green–yellow in colour. Male flowers are loose bunches of catkins
Habitat: Parks, large gardens, woodland and hedgerows
Fruits or seeds: Fruits called acorns grow inside cups
Flowering time: Spring

Acorn

Am I large? Does my bark have cracks in it? Are my leaves rounded and do I have acorns?

Common beech

Height: Up to 36 m
Types of flower: Separate male and female flowers that are green-white in colour. Single female flowers, and small clusters of male flowers
Habitat: Parks, large gardens, woodland and hedgerows
Fruits or seeds: Pairs of small, brown nuts in husks
Flowering time: Spring

Pine

Height: Up to 36 m
Types of flower: Separate male and female cones
Habitat: Parks, woodland, large gardens and forest, mainly in mountain areas
Fruits or seeds: Seeds in cones, which are scattered by the wind
Flowering time: Spring

Nut husk

Ripening cone

Male flower

Is my bark smooth and brown or grey? Are my broad leaves shiny green and do I have nut husks?

Am I evergreen with long needle-shaped leaves? Is my bark red-brown in colour?

Strange habits

A few plants have strange feeding habits. Some trap and eat small animals, while some steal food from other plants. There are even plants with flowers that are disguised as something else.

White berry

? Am I growing on one of the branches of a deciduous tree? Do I have green leaves and white, sticky berries?

Mistletoe
Height: Up to 90 cm
Size of flower: 2–4 mm
Flowers: In groups of 3–5
Habitat: Grows on the branches of deciduous trees
Fruits or seeds: Small sticky, white fruit
Flowering time: Autumn/winter

Spotting strange habits

- Some plants need more than sunlight, water and soil. They have to eat meat as well. The Venus flytrap has deadly leaves, which help to trap insects.

- Some orchids pretend to be flies, bees or wasps to attract insects to pollinate them.

- Mistletoe sinks its special roots into the branches of a tree to get some of its food.

- You may not find many strange plants growing in the wild, but they can often be found at garden centres.

Did you know?
The largest meat-eating plant in the world is a kind of pitcher plant. Its flowers can be up to one metre deep. It can catch and eat frogs.

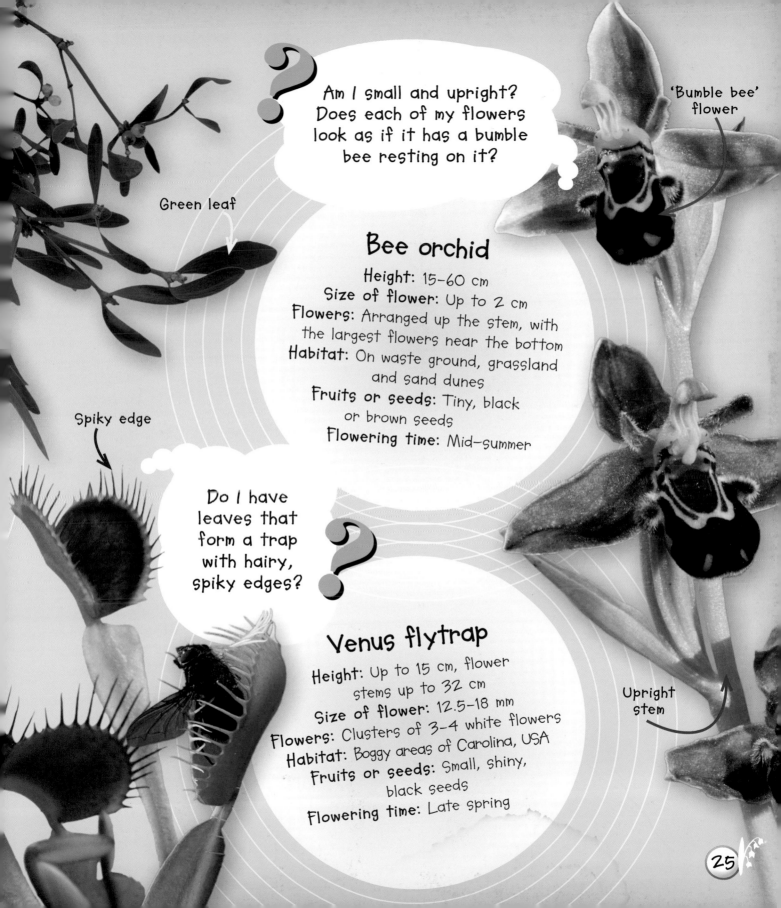

Green leaf

'Bumble bee' flower

Am I small and upright? Does each of my flowers look as if it has a bumble bee resting on it?

Bee orchid

Height: 15–60 cm
Size of flower: Up to 2 cm
Flowers: Arranged up the stem, with the largest flowers near the bottom
Habitat: On waste ground, grassland and sand dunes
Fruits or seeds: Tiny, black or brown seeds
Flowering time: Mid–summer

Spiky edge

Do I have leaves that form a trap with hairy, spiky edges?

Venus flytrap

Height: Up to 15 cm, flower stems up to 32 cm
Size of flower: 12.5–18 mm
Flowers: Clusters of 3–4 white flowers
Habitat: Boggy areas of Carolina, USA
Fruits or seeds: Small, shiny, black seeds
Flowering time: Late spring

Upright stem

Plants fight back

The leaves, flowers, fruits and seeds of plants are often eaten by animals. Some plants have special ways of protecting themselves.

Spotting plant defenders

✿ A large number of plants, including cacti, teasel, thistles, holly and brambles, use spines or thorns to protect themselves.

✿ A stinging nettle's stems and leaves are covered in tiny needle-like hairs. Below each hair is a tiny bag of poison. If you brush against the nettle plant, the poison is squeezed into your skin, causing a sting.

✿ Some plants, such as foxglove and ragwort, are poisonous to grazing animals. If an animal eats part of the plant, it will be sick or even die.

Do I have dark-green leaves with spines? Do I have small, white flowers and red berries?

White flower

Red berry

Dark-green leaf

Holly
Height: Up to 20 m
Size of flower: About 5 mm
Flowers: In clusters
Habitat: Gardens, hedgerows and woodland
Fruits or seeds: Red berries
Flowering time: Spring

Do I have leaves that are spoon shaped with rough edges? Am I covered in stinging hairs?

Do I grow tall and straight, with no branches? Are my flowers bell shaped?

Male flower

Bell-shaped flower

Spoon-shaped leaf

Stinging nettle

Height: 30–150 cm
Size of flower: About 2 mm
Flowers: Separate male and female plants
Habitat: Hedgerows, waste ground, gardens, woodland and forests
Fruits or seeds: Tiny, dry seeds
Flowering time: Summer/autumn

Foxglove

Height: 60–160 cm
Size of flower: 4–5 cm long
Flowers: Long spike with 20–80 flowers on a single stem
Habitat: Gardens and parks, hedgerows, woodland and forests
Fruits or seeds: Seeds in a pod
Flowering time: Summer

Plants in danger

Although plants seem to be almost everywhere, many kinds are in danger of dying out altogether. This is called **extinction**. Plants face extinction because of things that human beings do.

↑ This land is being cleared to make way for a new factory. Unless the plants that grow here have scattered their seeds to other areas, they will disappear from this area.

Habitat loss

Every kind of plant lives in particular surroundings. This is its **habitat**. All over the world, habitats are being destroyed. Soil is being covered over with concrete, tarmac and buildings. When their habitats are destroyed, the plants will have nowhere to grow.

Collecting wild plants

In some parts of the world, many beautiful wild plants have been dug up and sold to gardeners. Often the plants can only grow in their original habitats.

← People dug up so many wild orchids to plant in their gardens, the plant is now very rare in the wild.

Pollution

Many plants have been killed by chemicals used on farms and gardens to get rid of pests and kill weeds. Often this type of **pollution** kills not only the weeds, but also harmless wild plants growing nearby. If the chemicals do not kill the wild plants, they may kill the bees and other insects that pollinate them.

⬆ The chemical being sprayed on this field may kill trees, flowers and plants in a nearby hedge or wood.

Did you know?

Some species of orchid can have as many as 20,000 seeds in each capsule. The seeds are so tiny that three million of them only weigh one gram.

Watch it!

Everyone can do their bit to help wild plants by making the areas around homes and schools safe for plants to live. Even without a garden, we can plant pots, tubs or window boxes with the flowers that bees, butterflies and other insects like to visit. It is also important to take care of the soil by not putting anything on it that might damage plants.

Glossary

Bulb The underground stem that contains stored food.

Carpel The female parts of a flower.

Corm The swollen part of a stem that grows underground.

Deciduous Trees and bushes that lose their leaves in a certain season.

Evergreen Trees that do not lose their leaves in a certain season.

Extinction Not in existence any more. A species is extinct when no members of it are left alive.

Fertilization When a pollen grain reaches and joins with an egg-cell in a plant. Only a fertilized egg-cell can grow into a seed.

Habitat Where an animal or plant lives.

Nectar A sweet-tasting liquid produced by flowers.

Ovary The female part of a flower where the egg-cells and seeds are produced.

Petal One of the brightly coloured parts of a flower.

Pollen A yellow dust produced by flowers.

Pollination The carrying of pollen from one flower to another. This is usually done by insects or the wind.

Pollution Harmful substances that damage the environment.

Sepal The special leaf-like part of a flower that covers and protects the bud.

Species Any one kind of animal or plant.

Stamen One of the male parts of a flower. A stamen produces pollen.

Stigma The top of the female part of a flower, to which pollen grains stick.

Style The narrow part of a flower's carpel, which is underneath the stigma.

Index

Notes for parents and teachers

❀ Remember when you help a child to identify flowering plants, that only a tiny proportion of the total number of species can be shown in a book of this size. In the world as a whole, there are more than 350,000 species of wild plants, and many thousands more plant species and varieties have been developed to grow in gardens. Larger reference books containing clear pictures of wild or garden plants will prove very useful.

❀ The children should be encouraged to understand that it is against the law to dig up wild plants without the permission of the owner of the land. In addition, many rarer wildflowers are protected by law.

❀ A visit to a botanical garden, arboretum, large park, or to a natural history museum will help the children to appreciate the great diversity of plant life in the world today.

❀ A number of safety precautions are necessary when children study plants. They should always wash their hands thoroughly after handling plants and soil, particularly before touching food. If the children collect soil in which to grow seeds or plants, ensure that the soil comes from a part of the garden that has not been contaminated by dog or cat faeces and does not contain broken glass, nails or other sharp objects.

❀ Remember that some children are allergic to the juices of certain plants. If there is any doubt, the children should wear gloves when handling plants and soil. Some children are also allergic to the pollen from flowers.

❀ Always use plastic jars and other containers in preference to glass ones.

❀ Some useful websites for more information:
www.urbanext.uiuc.edu/gpe/
www.picadome.fcps.net/lab/currl/plants/default.htm
http://library.thinkquest.org/3715/
www.inhs.uiuc.edu/resources/tree_kit/student/index.html
www.sciencespot.net
www.kidzone.ws/plants

Website information is correct at time of going to press. However, the publishers cannot accept liability for any information or links found on third-party websites.